The
Bedtime
Sh'ma

A Good Night Book

לַיְלָה טוב
קְרִיאַת שְׁמַע עַל הַמִּטָה

The Bedtime Sh'ma

A Good Night Book

לַיְלָה טוֹב

קְרִיאַת שְׁמַע עַל הַמִּטָּה

Adapted by Sarah Gershman

Illustrated by Kristina Swarner

EKS PUBLISHING CO.
Oakland, California

In loving memory of Beth Samuels

The Bedtime Sh'ma: A Good Night Book

Copyright © 2007 by Sarah Gershman

Printed in The United States

EKS Publishing Co.
PO Box 9750
Berkeley, CA 94709-0750
email: orders@ekspublishing.com
Phone: (510) 251-9100
Fax: (510) 251-9102

ISBN 978-0-939144-54-9
Third Printing, November 2008

Library of Congress Cataloging-in-Publication Data:

Gershman, Sarah, 1972-
The bedtime Sh'ma : a good night book = [Lailah tov : keri'at ha-Shema' 'al ha-mitah] / adapted by Sarah Gershman ; illustrated by Kristina Swarner.
    p.   cm.
Includes the text of selections from the Shema in English and Hebrew.
ISBN 978-0-939144-54-9 (pbk.) — ISBN 978-0-939144-55-6
1. Shema—Juvenile literature. 2. Judaism—Liturgy—Texts.
3. Jewish children—Prayers and devotions. 4. Bedtime prayers—Juvenile literature.
I. Swarner, Kristina. II. Shema. III. Shema. English & Hebrew. Selections.
IV. Title. V. Title: Lailah tov.
BM670.S45G47 2007
296.4'5—dc22
2007060519

What have I done today?

Did I hurt someone else? I ask forgiveness.

Did someone hurt me? I try to forgive.

Thank you God for giving me
eyes that close so that I may rest.
I hope my dreams are sweet tonight.

My child, may you lay down gently to sleep.

And may God's peace spread over you.

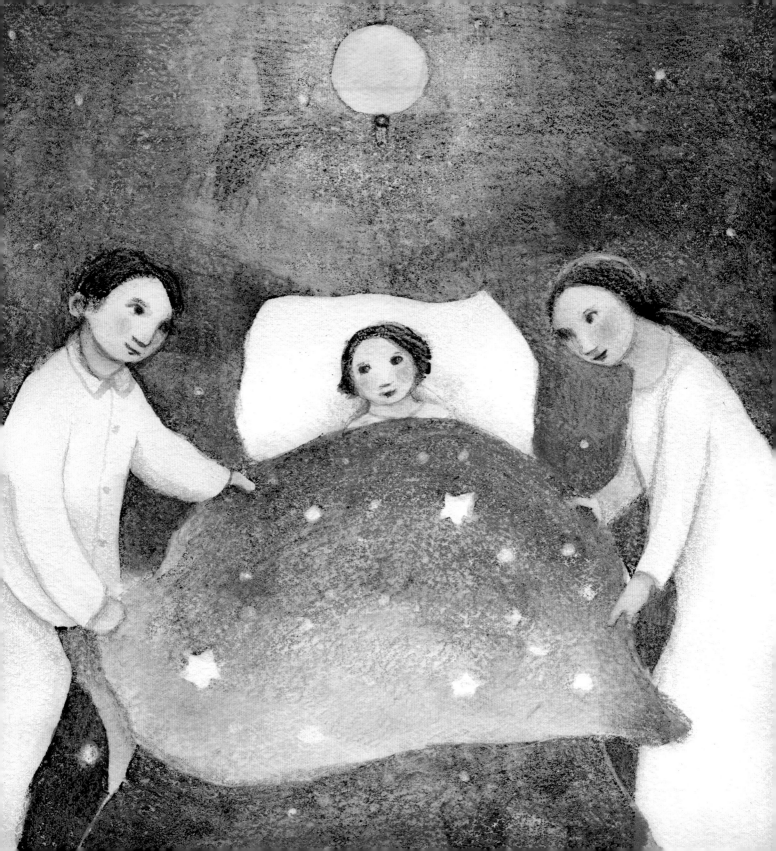

May God who watched over those who were here long ago, watch over you.

May God bless you and keep you safe.

May God give you light when it is dark.

May God help you grow and be happy.

It is time to sleep, but I am not alone.

Wonder is at my right.
Tomorrow will be filled
with new adventures.

Strength is at my left.

When I sleep, my body grows stronger.

Light is behind me.

I am safe in the dark.

Comfort is in front of me.

I feel warm and sleepy.

Sh'ma Yisrael Adonai Eloheinu Adonai Echad

Listen Israel. God is our God. God is One.

Baruch shem k'vod malchuto l'olam va'ed

How wonderful is God's world.

I rest myself in God's hand.

God is with me and I am not afraid.

קְרִיאַת שְׁמַע עַל הַמִּטָּה

Excerpts from the Bedtime Sh'ma

רִבּוֹנוֹ שֶׁל עוֹלָם, הֲרֵינִי מוֹחֵל לְכָל מִי שֶׁהִכְעִיס וְהִקְנִיט אוֹתִי, אוֹ שֶׁחָטָא כְּנֶגְדִּי, בֵּין בְּגוּפִי בֵּין בְּמָמוֹנִי, בֵּין בִּכְבוֹדִי בֵּין בְּכָל אֲשֶׁר לִי, בֵּין בְּאֹנֶס בֵּין בְּרָצוֹן, בֵּין בְּשׁוֹגֵג בֵּין בְּמֵזִיד, בֵּין בְּדִבּוּר בֵּין בְּמַעֲשֶׂה, בֵּין בְּמַחֲשָׁבָה בֵּין בְּהִרְהוּר, בֵּין בְּגִלְגּוּל זֶה בֵּין בְּגִלְגּוּל אַחֵר, לְכָל בַּר יִשְׂרָאֵל, וְלֹא יֵעָנֵשׁ שׁוּם אָדָם בְּסִבָּתִי. יְהִי רָצוֹן מִלְּפָנֶיךָ, יְיָ אֱלֹהַי וֵאלֹהֵי אֲבוֹתַי, שֶׁלֹּא אֶחֱטָא עוֹד, וּמַה שֶּׁחָטָאתִי לְפָנֶיךָ מְחוֹק בְּרַחֲמֶיךָ הָרַבִּים, אֲבָל לֹא עַל יְדֵי יִסּוּרִים וָחֳלָיִים רָעִים. יִהְיוּ לְרָצוֹן אִמְרֵי פִי וְהֶגְיוֹן לִבִּי לְפָנֶיךָ, יְיָ צוּרִי וְגֹאֲלִי.

Master of the Universe, I forgive anyone who made me angry or upset or who hurt me, my body, my things, my feelings, or anything that is mine, whether by accident or on purpose, by words, actions or thoughts, in this world or in another world. I forgive each one. May no one be punished because of me. May it be your will God – God of my ancestors – that I not hurt anyone anymore. Whatever hurt that I have done, may you forgive me and not punish me. May these words I say and these feelings in my heart make you happy, God, my rock and my redeemer.

בָּרוּךְ אַתָּה יְיָ אֱלֹהֵינוּ מֶלֶךְ הָעוֹלָם, הַמַּפִּיל חֶבְלֵי שֵׁנָה עַל עֵינַי, וּתְנוּמָה עַל עַפְעַפָּי. וִיהִי רָצוֹן מִלְּפָנֶיךָ, יְיָ אֱלֹהַי וֵאלֹהֵי אֲבוֹתַי, שֶׁתַּשְׁכִּיבֵנִי לְשָׁלוֹם, וְתַעֲמִידֵנִי לְשָׁלוֹם, וְאַל יְבַהֲלוּנִי רַעְיוֹנַי וַחֲלוֹמוֹת רָעִים וְהִרְהוּרִים רָעִים, וּתְהֵא מִטָּתִי שְׁלֵמָה לְפָנֶיךָ, וְהָאֵר עֵינַי פֶּן אִישַׁן הַמָּוֶת, כִּי אַתָּה הַמֵּאִיר לְאִישׁוֹן בַּת עָיִן. בָּרוּךְ אַתָּה יְיָ, הַמֵּאִיר לָעוֹלָם כֻּלּוֹ בִּכְבוֹדוֹ.

Blessed are you God, our God, Ruler of the world who makes my eyes heavy and my eyelids sleepy. May it be your will God, God of my ancestors, that I lay down to sleep in peace and awake in peace. May I not be upset by any bad dreams or thoughts. May my children someday make you happy. May you help me see in the dark, for it is you who illuminates the pupil of the eye. Blessed are you God, who lights up the whole world with your glory.

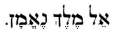

God the Faithful Ruler.

שְׁמַע יִשְׂרָאֵל, יְיָ אֱלֹהֵינוּ, יְיָ אֶחָד.

Listen Israel, God is our God. God is One.

בָּרוּךְ שֵׁם כְּבוֹד מַלְכוּתוֹ לְעוֹלָם וָעֶד.

Blessed is the Name of God's Kingdom forever and ever.

וְאָהַבְתָּ אֵת יְיָ אֱלֹהֶיךָ, בְּכָל לְבָבְךָ, וּבְכָל נַפְשְׁךָ, וּבְכָל מְאֹדֶךָ. וְהָיוּ הַדְּבָרִים הָאֵלֶּה,
אֲשֶׁר אָנֹכִי מְצַוְּךָ הַיּוֹם, עַל לְבָבֶךָ. וְשִׁנַּנְתָּם לְבָנֶיךָ, וְדִבַּרְתָּ בָּם, בְּשִׁבְתְּךָ בְּבֵיתֶךָ,
וּבְלֶכְתְּךָ בַדֶּרֶךְ, וּבְשָׁכְבְּךָ, וּבְקוּמֶךָ. וּקְשַׁרְתָּם לְאוֹת עַל יָדֶךָ, וְהָיוּ לְטֹטָפֹת בֵּין עֵינֶיךָ.
וּכְתַבְתָּם עַל מְזֻזוֹת בֵּיתֶךָ וּבִשְׁעָרֶיךָ.

And you shall love God, your God, with all your heart, with all your soul, and with everything
that you have. May you take to heart these things that I command you today. Teach them to your
children. Speak of them when you sit in your house and when you walk on your way, when you lie
down, and when you rise up. Put them as a sign on your arm and *tefillin* between your eyes. Write
them on the doorposts of your house and on your gates.

וִיהִי נֹעַם אֲדֹנָי אֱלֹהֵינוּ עָלֵינוּ, וּמַעֲשֵׂה יָדֵינוּ כּוֹנְנָה עָלֵינוּ, וּמַעֲשֵׂה יָדֵינוּ כּוֹנְנֵהוּ.

May the sweetness of God, our God, be upon us. And [may God] give intention to the work of our
hands, and the work of our hands give meaning to God.

הַשְׁכִּיבֵנוּ יְיָ אֱלֹהֵינוּ לְשָׁלוֹם, וְהַעֲמִידֵנוּ מַלְכֵּנוּ לְחַיִּים, וּפְרוֹשׂ עָלֵינוּ סֻכַּת שְׁלוֹמֶךָ,
וְתַקְּנֵנוּ בְּעֵצָה טוֹבָה מִלְּפָנֶיךָ, וְהוֹשִׁיעֵנוּ לְמַעַן שְׁמֶךָ. וְהָגֵן בַּעֲדֵנוּ, וְהָסֵר מֵעָלֵינוּ אוֹיֵב,
דֶּבֶר, וְחֶרֶב, וְרָעָב, וְיָגוֹן, וְהָסֵר שָׂטָן מִלְּפָנֵינוּ וּמֵאַחֲרֵינוּ, וּבְצֵל כְּנָפֶיךָ תַּסְתִּירֵנוּ, כִּי אֵל
שׁוֹמְרֵנוּ וּמַצִּילֵנוּ אַתָּה, כִּי אֵל מֶלֶךְ חַנּוּן וְרַחוּם אָתָּה, וּשְׁמוֹר צֵאתֵנוּ וּבוֹאֵנוּ, לְחַיִּים
וּלְשָׁלוֹם, מֵעַתָּה וְעַד עוֹלָם.

Lay us down to sleep in peace and raise us up in life, our Ruler. Spread over us the shelter of your
peace. Set us right with your counsel and by being in your presence. And save us for your name's
sake. Shield us, protect us from enemies, plague, violence, hunger, and sorrow. Remove obstacles
in front of and behind us and shelter us under the shadow of your wings. For you are God, who
protects and rescues us; you are a gracious and compassionate Lord. Guard our going and coming –
for life and for peace, from now and forever more.

הַמַּלְאָךְ הַגֹּאֵל אֹתִי מִכָּל רָע יְבָרֵךְ אֶת הַנְּעָרִים, וְיִקָּרֵא בָהֶם שְׁמִי וְשֵׁם אֲבוֹתַי אַבְרָהָם וְיִצְחָק, וְיִדְגּוּ לָרֹב בְּקֶרֶב הָאָרֶץ.

May the angel who saves me from evil bless these children and may my name be declared through them – and the name of my forefathers Abraham and Isaac – and may they become abundant like fish within the land.

יְבָרֶכְךָ יי וְיִשְׁמְרֶךָ. יָאֵר יי פָּנָיו אֵלֶיךָ וִיחֻנֶּךָּ. יִשָּׂא יי פָּנָיו אֵלֶיךָ וְיָשֵׂם לְךָ שָׁלוֹם.

May God bless you and keep you safe. May God shine God's presence on you and be gracious to you. May God turn God's face towards you and give you peace.

בְּשֵׁם יי אֱלֹהֵי יִשְׂרָאֵל, מִימִינִי מִיכָאֵל, וּמִשְּׂמֹאלִי גַּבְרִיאֵל, וּמִלְּפָנַי אוּרִיאֵל, וּמֵאֲחוֹרַי רְפָאֵל, וְעַל רֹאשִׁי שְׁכִינַת אֵל.

In the name of God, God of Israel: Michael is at my right, Gabriel is at my left, Uriel is in front of me, and Raphael is behind me. And above my head is the Presence of God.

אֲדוֹן עוֹלָם אֲשֶׁר מָלַךְ, בְּטֶרֶם כָּל יְצִיר נִבְרָא. לְעֵת נַעֲשָׂה בְחֶפְצוֹ כֹּל, אֲזַי מֶלֶךְ שְׁמוֹ נִקְרָא. וְאַחֲרֵי כִּכְלוֹת הַכֹּל, לְבַדּוֹ יִמְלוֹךְ נוֹרָא. וְהוּא הָיָה, וְהוּא הֹוֶה, וְהוּא יִהְיֶה, בְּתִפְאָרָה. וְהוּא אֶחָד וְאֵין שֵׁנִי, לְהַמְשִׁיל לוֹ לְהַחְבִּירָה. בְּלִי רֵאשִׁית בְּלִי תַכְלִית, וְלוֹ הָעֹז וְהַמִּשְׂרָה. וְהוּא אֵלִי וְחַי גֹּאֲלִי, וְצוּר חֶבְלִי בְּעֵת צָרָה. וְהוּא נִסִּי וּמָנוֹס לִי, מְנָת כּוֹסִי בְּיוֹם אֶקְרָא. בְּיָדוֹ אַפְקִיד רוּחִי, בְּעֵת אִישָׁן וְאָעִירָה. וְעִם רוּחִי גְּוִיָּתִי, יי לִי וְלֹא אִירָא.

Ruler of the universe who ruled before any form of creation, when God brought everything into being – then as "Sovereign" was God's name proclaimed. And after all has ended, God, the Awesome One will rule. It is God who was, and God who is, and God who will be, in glory. God is one, and there is no other to compare to God or equal God. God has neither beginning nor end. God is power and dominion. God is my God, my living savior, the rock of my pain in the time of my suffering. God is my banner and my refuge, the portion in my cup on the day I call. In God's hand I will rest my spirit when I sleep and I will wake up. My body will stay with my spirit. God is with me and I will not be afraid.

About the Bedtime Sh'ma

Reading stories to children is one of the oldest and most beloved bedtime rituals. "Good night" books help children unwind and feel safe before going to sleep. The sages of Jewish tradition understood the power of bedtime and wisely put together a Jewish "good night book" in the form of the *Kriat Sh'ma al haMitah,* the Bedtime *Sh'ma.*

The Bedtime *Sh'ma* is a collection of psalms, poems and prayers that focus on the themes of protection and preparing for sleep. This book is an interpretation of excerpts of the actual liturgy. The full text of those excerpts is included in Hebrew and English in the back of the book. I have tried to stay true to the essence of the prayer, while interpreting the ancient texts with the youngest of listeners in mind.

In the first paragraph of the *Sh'ma*, we are told to speak these words "when you lie down and when you rise." Consequently, the *Sh'ma* is traditionally recited both at night and in the morning. In *Tractate Brachot* of the Babylonian Talmud, it states that saying the *Sh'ma* right before sleep serves as a protection from the dangers of the night.

In the modern age of electricity, we can lose sight of how frightening and dark the night really is. It is often children who remind us what it means to be "scared of the dark." The Bedtime *Sh'ma* recognizes these feelings of vulnerability, while reminding us of the wonder that our bodies come to rest each night and awaken each morning.

Laila Tov, Good Night!

Sarah Gershman